# Quick-and-Easy Christmas Crochet

## by Barbara Christopher

DOVER PUBLICATIONS, INC., *New York*

With love
to a very special friend

Copyright © 1991 by Dover Publications, Inc.
All rights reserved under Pan American and International Copyright Conventions.

Published in Canada by General Publishing Company, Ltd., 30 Lesmill Road, Don Mills, Toronto, Ontario.
Published in the United Kingdom by Constable and Company, Ltd., 3 The Lanchesters, 162–164 Fulham Palace Road, London W6 9ER.

*Quick-and-Easy Christmas Crochet* is a new work, first published by Dover Publications, Inc., in 1991.

Manufactured in the United States of America
Dover Publications, Inc., 31 East 2nd Street, Mineola, N.Y. 11501

*Library of Congress Cataloging-in-Publication Data*

Christopher, Barbara.
    Quick-and-easy Christmas crochet / by Barbara Christopher.
        p.    cm. — (Dover needlework series)
    ISBN 0-486-26805-5 (pbk.)
    1. Crocheting—Patterns.  2. Christmas decorations.  I. Title.
II. Series.
TT820.C497   1991
745.594′12—dc20                                            91-2641
                                                             CIP

# Introduction

To me, there is nothing more festive than a tree or wreath accented with crisp white crocheted ornaments; and there is nothing I enjoy more than creating delicate, lacy decorations for the holidays. I had so much fun doing my first crochet book, *60 Crocheted Snowflakes*, that I decided to try another. In this collection of 50 ornaments I have included stars, angels, three-dimensional bells and balls, as well as a totally new supply of snowflakes.

The ornaments are all made using DMC threads*— two sizes of Cebelia and one size of pearl cotton. Because of space limitations, the ornaments are shown slightly smaller than actual size; an approximate size is given with each instruction. I have listed the size crochet hook I used for each ornament, but you may find that you need to use a larger or smaller hook to make the ornament the size stated. If you decide to make the ornament a different size, you can do so by simply changing the thread and hook size you use. Just remember that the ornaments look best if they are crocheted tightly.

On some ornaments, I have added additional sparkle by using Balger ⅛"-wide metallic ribbon. For information on where to obtain Balger ribbons, write to Kreinik Manufacturing Co., Inc., P.O. Box 1966, Parkersburg, WV 26102.

All ornaments must be blocked and starched after they are completed. If your work is soiled, wash it in warm water with a mild soap. Rinse it thoroughly and roll it in a towel to remove the excess moisture.

A number of different products can be used to stiffen the ornament. Commercial lace stiffeners are available, but "homemade" solutions work just as well. One possibility is to dilute white craft glue with an equal amount of water. The traditional, although somewhat messy, choice is sugar starch. To make it, mix equal amounts of sugar and water in a small pan. Bring the mixture to a rapid boil, then let it cool to room temperature. I generally use a thick solution of commercial boilable starch. Don't use spray or liquid starch; they won't give the piece enough body.

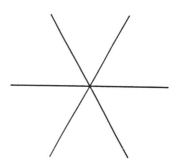

**Snowflake Blocking Guide**

**Star Blocking Guide**

Fill a bowl with the stiffening solution and immerse the crocheted piece for several minutes. Take it out and gently press out the excess solution—the piece should still be very wet. Place flat pieces right side up on a plastic-covered pinning board (I use a piece of pressed cardboard). Using rust-proof pins, carefully pin the piece to shape, starting at the center and pinning each picot in place. To make blocking snowflakes and stars easier, I have included a blocking guide for each.†

*For information on where to obtain DMC threads, write to the DMC Corporation, Port Kearny Building #10, South Kearny, NJ 07032-0650.

†Snowflake blocking guide used with the permission of the American School of Needlework, Inc., ASN Publishing, 1455 Linda Vista Drive, San Marcos, CA 92069.

Trace the appropriate guide onto tissue or tracing paper and extend the arms out to the finished size of the piece. Place the guide under the plastic on the pinning board. As you pin, align the points with the arms of the guide. Let the piece dry thoroughly before removing the pins.

Blocking three-dimensional ornaments is a little trickier, but can be done using some readily available "props." Insert a small balloon into each ball after you remove it from the starch. Inflate the balloon to shape the ball and tie it securely. After the ball is dry, either pop the balloon or untie it.

For the angels, make a cone from lightweight card-board. The cone should be about the height of the angel and the bottom should be the same diameter as the lower edge of the angel. Cut off the tip of the cone so that the top is about 1″ in diameter. Cover the cone with plastic wrap. Starch the angel's body (don't im-merse the stuffed head in the starch) and shape it over the cone. Starch and shape the wings and arms, then sew them to the body.

To make a form for each bell, wad and shape plastic wrap with your hands; tape securely. Starch the bell, then shape it over the form. After the bell is dry, tie the clapper to the inside top of the bell.

## *Abbreviations*

| | |
|---|---|
| beg | beginning |
| bet | between |
| ch(s) | chain(s) |
| ch-sp | chain space |
| dc | double crochet |
| dtr | double treble crochet (yo hook 3 times) |
| hdc | half double crochet |
| lp(s) | loop(s) |
| rep | repeat |
| rnd | round |
| sc | single crochet |
| sl st(s) | slip stitch(es) |
| sp(s) | spaces |
| st(s) | stitch(es) |
| tr | treble crochet |
| yo | yarn over |

*, ** or † Repeat the instructions following the symbol or enclosed by two symbols the specified number of times.

[  ] Repeat the instructions enclosed within the brackets the specified number of times.

## Snowflake #1 ◄

Approximately 3¼″ diameter

### Materials
DMC Cebelia #20, 9 yds.
Size 10 steel crochet hook.

Ch 20; join with sl st in first sc to form ring.
**Rnd 1:** Ch 3, work 35 dc in ring; join in top of beg ch 3.
**Rnd 2:** *Ch 7, skip next 2 dc, tr in next dc, ch 7, skip next 2 dc, sl st in next dc. Rep from * 5 times, ending last rep with sl st in base of beg ch 7.
**Rnd 3:** Ch 1, *work 7 sc in next ch-7 sp, sc in tr, ch 12, sc in same tr, work 7 sc in next ch-7 sp, sl st in next sl st. Rep from * 5 times, ending last rep with sl st in beg ch 1.
**Rnd 4:** *[Sl st in next sc, ch 1] 7 times, [sl st in ch-12 lp, ch 1] 4 times, sl st in same lp, *ch 6, sl st in 6th ch from hook for large picot*, [ch 1, work large picot] twice, sl st in base of first large picot, [sl st in same ch-12 lp, ch 1] 5 times, [sl st in next sc, ch 1] 6 times, sl st in next sc, sl st in next sl st, work large picot, sl st in same sl st. Rep from * 5 times. Fasten off.

For a three-dimensional effect, push the single large picot and the lower part of each scallop forward.

## Snowflake #2 ►

Approximately 2½″ diameter

### Materials
DMC Cebelia #20, 8 yds.
Size 10 steel crochet hook.

Ch 5; join with sl st in first ch to form ring.
**Rnd 1:** Ch 3, work 17 dc in ring; join in top of beg ch 3.
**Rnd 2:** *Ch 4, tr in same sp, skip next st, tr in next st, ch 4, sl st in same st, sl st in next st. Rep from * 5 times—6 points.
**Rnd 3:** *Ch 7, tr bet ch 4 and the first tr of point, ch 7, tr bet the 2 tr of the point, ch 7, sl st bet the 2nd tr and the ch 4; ch 7, sl st bet the points. Rep from * 5 times.
**Rnd 4:** Sl st to center of 2nd ch-7 sp of point, sc in same sp, *ch 7, sc in next ch-7 sp, ch 12, skip next 2 ch-7 sps, sc in next ch-7 sp. Rep from * 5 times, ending last rep with a sl st in first sc of rnd. Fasten off.

## Snowflake #3 ◄

Approximately 3½″ diameter

### Materials
DMC pearl cotton #5, 10½ yds.
Size 4 steel crochet hook.

Ch 12; join with sl st in first ch to form ring.
**Rnd 1:** Ch 2, work 23 hdc in ring; join in top of beg ch 2.
**Rnd 2:** *Ch 11 loosely, sc in 2nd ch from hook, hdc in next ch, dc in next ch, tr in next ch, tr in each of next 2 chs, tr in next ch, dc in next ch, hdc in next ch, sc in last ch, sl st in each of next 4 sc. Rep from * 5 times—6 points.
**Rnd 3:** *Working around point, sc in each of 9 sts, 3 sc in tip of point, sc in each of next 9 sts, skip next sl st on ring, sl st in each of next 2 sl sts, skip next sl st on ring. Rep from * 5 times, sl st in first sc of rnd. Fasten off.

5

## Snowflake #4 ▲

Approximately 5″ diameter

### Materials
DMC Cebelia #10, 16 yds.
Size 7 steel crochet hook.

Ch 9; join with sl st in first ch to form ring.
**Rnd 1:** Ch 2, work 17 hdc in ring, join in top of beg ch 2.
**Rnd 2:** Ch 3 (counts as dc), dc in same sp, 2 dc in each hdc around; join in top of beg ch 3—36 dc.
**Rnd 3:** Sc in same sp, ch 6, skip next st, dtr in each of next 2 sts, ch 6, skip next st, sc in next st, [sc in next st, ch 6, skip next st, dtr in each of next 2 sts, ch 6, skip next st, sc in next st] 5 times, sl st in first sc—6 points.
**Rnd 4:** Sc bet first 2 sc, *ch 9, dc bet 2 dtr of next point, ch 9, sc bet 2 sc bet points; rep from * 5 times, ending last rep with sl st in first sc.
**Rnd 5:** Sc in same sp, *ch 11, dc in next dc, ch 11, sc in next sc; rep from * 5 times, ending last rep with sl st in first sc.
**Rnd 6:** Sc in same sp, *[ch 7, sl st in 7th ch from hook for picot] 3 times, sl st in sc just made, ch 13, dc in dc, work 3 picots, sl st in dc just made, ch 13, sc in next sc. Rep from * 5 times, ending last rep with sl st in first sc. Fasten off.

### ◄ Snowflake #5

Approximately 4″ diameter

**Materials**
DMC pearl cotton #5, 12 yds.
Size 4 steel crochet hook.

Ch 10; join with sl st in first ch to form ring.
**Rnd 1:** Ch 4 (counts as tr), 2 tr in ring, ch 3, [3 tr in ring, ch 3] 5 times, join in top of ch 4—6 tr groups.
**Rnd 2:** *[Ch 5, tr in center tr of same group, ch 5, sl st in last tr of group, ch 5, sl st in first tr of next group; rep from * 5 times, ending last rep with sl st in joining sl st of previous rnd.
**Rnd 3:** *Ch 9, tr in next tr, ch 9, sl st in next sl st, ch 3, sc in next ch-5 sp, ch 3, sl st in next sl st; rep from * 5 times.
**Rnd 4:** *Ch 2, *ch 5, sl st in 5th ch from hook for picot*, [ch 1, work picot] twice, ch 2, dc in next tr, work picot, sl st in dc just made, ch 2, [work picot, ch 1] twice, work picot, ch 2, sl st in sl st at base of point, sc in next ch-3 sp, work picot, sc in next ch-3 sp, sl st in sl st at base of next point. Rep from * 5 times. Fasten off.

### ◄ Snowflake #6

Approximately 2¾″ diameter

**Materials**
DMC Cebelia #10, 16 yds.
Size 7 steel crochet hook.

Ch 12; join with sl st in first ch to form ring.
**Rnd 1:** Work 24 sc in ring; join in first sc.
**Rnd 2:** Working in front lps of sts only, sc and dc in same st, dc and sc in next st, [sc and dc in next st, dc and sc in next st] 11 times, join in first sc.
**Rnd 3:** Sl st in back lp of first st of Rnd 1; working in back lps of Rnd 1 sts, [ch 12, skip next 2 sts, sl st in each of next 2 sts] 6 times.
**Rnd 4:** [Work 24 sc in next ch-12 lp, sl st bet lps] 6 times.
**Rnd 5:** Working in backs of sts, sl st to first free st of Rnd 1; sl st in this st and in next st, ch 20, [sl st in each of next 2 free sts, ch 20] 5 times, sl st in base of first ch 20.
**Rnd 6:** [Work 34 sc in next ch-20 lp, sl st bet ch 20 lps] 6 times. Fasten off.

*Snowflake #7*

*Snowflake #8*

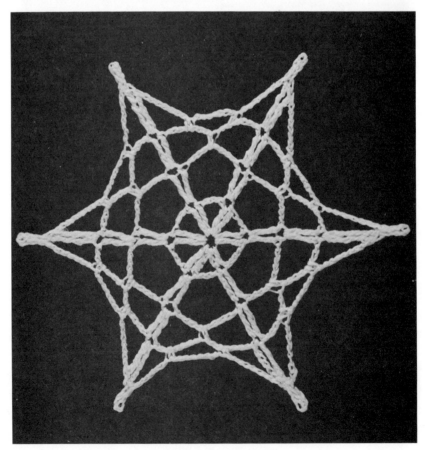

8

# ◄ Snowflake #7

Approximately 4¼″ diameter

**Materials**
DMC Cebelia #10, 15 yds.
Size 7 steel crochet hook.

Ch 7; join with sl st in first ch to form ring.
**Rnd 1:** Work 12 sc in ring; join in first sc.
**Rnd 2:** Ch 3 (counts as dc), dc in same sp, 2 dc in next sc, ch 2, [2 dc in each of next 2 sc, ch 2] 5 times; join in top of beg ch 3.
**Rnd 3:** Ch 3, dc in next dc, ch 2, dc in each of next 2 dc, ch 3, [dc in each of next 2 dc, ch 2, dc in each of next 2 dc, ch 3] 5 times; join in top of beg ch 3.
**Rnd 4:** Ch 3, dc in next dc, ch 3, dc in each of next 2 dc, ch 6, [dc in each of next 2 dc, ch 3, dc in each of next 2 dc, ch 6] 5 times; join in top of beg ch 3.
**Rnd 5:** Ch 3, dc in next dc, ch 4, dc in each of next 2 dc, ch 8, [dc in each of next 2 dc, ch 4, dc in each of next 2 dc, ch 8] 5 times; join in top of beg ch 3.
**Rnd 6:** Ch 3, dc in next dc, 2 dc in next ch-4 sp, dc in each of next 2 dc, ch 7, sc in next ch-7 sp, ch 7, *dc in each of next 2 dc, 2 dc in next ch-4 sp, dc in each of next 2 dc, ch 7, sc in next ch-7 sp, ch 7. Rep from * 4 times; join in top of beg ch 3.
**Rnd 7:** Ch 4, *yo twice and draw up a lp in next dc, [yo and draw through 2 lps] twice;* rep bet *s 4 times, yo and draw through all 6 lps on hook to complete starting cluster, [ch 9, sc in next ch-7 sp] twice, ch 9, †rep bet *s 6 times, yo and draw through all 7 lps on hook to complete cluster, [ch 9, sc in next ch-7 sp] twice, ch 9. Rep from † 4 times; join in top of beg ch 4. Fasten off.

# ◄ Snowflake #8

Approximately 5″ diameter

**Materials**
DMC pearl cotton #5, 9½ yds.
Size 4 steel crochet hook.

**Rnd 1:** Ch 5, tr in 5th ch from hook, ch 3, [2 tr in same sp, ch 3] 5 times, sl st in sp before first tr.
**Rnd 2:** Ch 4, tr in same sp, ch 9, [2 tr in sp bet next 2 tr, ch 9] 5 times, sl st in sp before first tr.
**Rnd 3:** Ch 4, tr in sp before first tr, ch 7, sc in ch-9 sp, ch 7, [2 tr in sp bet next 2 tr, ch 7, sc in next ch-9 sp, ch 7] 5 times, sl st in sp before first tr.
**Rnd 4:** Ch 5, *ch 6, sl st in 6th ch from hook for picot*, dtr in sp before first tr, [ch 7, sc in next ch-7 sp] twice, ch 7, *dtr in sp bet next 2 tr, work picot, dtr in same sp as last dtr, [ch 7, sc in next ch-7 sp] twice, ch 7. Rep from * 4 times, join in top of beg ch 5. Fasten off.

# Snowflake #9 ▲

Approximately 3⅝″ diameter

**Materials**
DMC Cebelia #20, 14 yds.
Size 10 steel crochet hook.

Ch 7; join with sl st in first ch to form ring.
**Rnd 1:** Ch 3 (counts as dc), dc in ring, ch 3, [2 dc in ring, ch 3] 5 times, join in top of beg ch 3.
**Rnd 2:** Ch 5, work starting cluster as follows: *yo 3 times, draw up a lp in same sp, [yo and draw through 2 lps] 3 times;* rep bet *s 3 times in next st, yo and draw through all 5 lps on hook, ch 10, †work cluster as follows: rep bet *s twice in next dc, rep bet *s 3 times in next dc, yo and draw through all 6 lps on hook, ch 10. Rep from † 4 times, join in top of starting cluster.
**Rnd 3:** Sc in top of same cluster, *in next ch-10 sp, work 2 sc, 2 hdc, 2 dc, tr, 2 dtr, tr, 2 dc, 2 hdc, 2 sc; sc in top of next cluster. Rep from * around, ending last rep with sl st in top of first sc— 6 points.
**Rnd 4:** Ch 5, work starting cluster as follows: *yo 3 times and draw up a lp in same sp, [yo and draw through 2 lps] 3 times;* rep bet *s 3 times, yo and draw through all 5 lps on hook; [ch 9, sl st in 9th ch from hook for large picot] 3 times, sl st in cluster just made, ch 10, sc bet 2 tr at tip of next point, work picot as before, sc in same sp as last sc, ch 10, †work cluster as follows: rep bet *s 5 times in sc bet points, yo and draw through all 6 lps on hook; work 3 picots, sl st in top of cluster just made, ch 10, sc bet 2 tr at tip of next point, work picot, sc in same sp as last sc, ch 10. Rep from † around, join in top of starting cluster. Fasten off.

### ◄ *Snowflake #10*

Approximately 1½″ diameter

**Materials**
DMC Cebelia #20, 3½ yds.
Size 10 steel crochet hook.

Ch 7; join with sl st in first ch to form ring.
**Rnd 1:** Work 12 sc in ring; join in first sc.
**Rnd 2:** [Ch 5, skip next sc, sl st in next st] 6 times—6 points.
**Rnd 3:** *Ch 2, *ch 4, sl st in 4th ch from hook for small picot,* ch 1, *ch 6, sl st in 6th ch from hook for large picot,* ch 1, work small picot, ch 2, sl st in sl st bet points. Rep from * 5 times; fasten off.

### *Snowflake #11* ►

Approximately 1¾″ diameter

**Materials**
DMC Cebelia #10, 4 yds.
Size 7 steel crochet hook.

Ch 9; join with sl st in first ch to form ring.
**Rnd 1:** Ch 2; work 23 hdc in ring; join in top of beg ch 2.
**Rnd 2:** [Sc in next st, ch 6, skip next 2 sts, sc in next st] 6 times, sl st in first sc.
**Rnd 3:** Sc in same sp, *in next ch-6 sp, work [sc in sp, *ch 4, sl st in 4th ch from hook for picot*] 3 times, sc in same sp, skip next sc, sc in next sc. Rep from * 5 times, ending last rep with sl st in first sc. Fasten off.

### ◄ *Snowflake #12*

Approximately 4″ diameter

**Materials**
DMC Cebelia #10, 11½ yds.
Size 7 steel crochet hook.

Ch 10; join with sl st in first ch to form ring.
**Rnd 1:** Ch 3 (counts as dc), 2 dc in ring, *ch 5, sl st in 5th ch from hook for picot,* [4 dc in ring, work picot] 5 times, dc in ring; join in top of beg ch 3.
**Rnd 2:** Sc in sp before next dc, ch 10, [skip picot, sc bet center 2 dc of next 4-dc group, ch 10] 5 times; join in first sc.
**Rnd 3:** Sc in same sp, *work 4 picots, sl st in 2nd picot made, work picot, sl st in next picot, sl st in last sc worked in, 6 sc in ch-10 lp, work 6 picots, sl st in 4th picot, [work picot, sl st in next picot] 3 times, 6 sc in ch-10 lp, sc in next sc. Rep from * 5 times, ending last rep with sl st in first sc of rnd. Fasten off.

## Snowflake #14 ▶

Approximately 2½″ diameter

### Materials
DMC Cebelia #20, 10 yds.
Size 10 steel crochet hook.

Ch 9; join with sl st in first ch to form ring.
**Rnd 1:** Ch 2, work 23 hdc in ring; join in top of beg ch 2.
**Rnd 2:** Working in front lps of sts, [sc in next sc, ch 5, skip next sc] 12 times; join in first sc.
**Rnd 3:** Sc in same sc, *in next ch-5 lp, work sl st, ch 1 and sl st, *ch 5, sl st in 5th ch from hook for picot*, work sl st, ch 1 and sl st in same ch-5 lp. Rep from * around, ending last rep with sl st in first sc of rnd.
**Rnd 4:** Sl st to back lp of first st of Rnd 1; working in back lps, sc in first sc worked in on Rnd 2, ch 12, skip next sc, *sc in next sc, ch 12, skip next sc. Rep from * around; join in first sc of rnd.
**Rnd 5:** Sc in same sc, *in next ch-12 lp, work [sl st and ch 1] 3 times, sl st in same lp, work picot, in same lp work [sl st and ch 1] 3 times, sl st in same lp, sc in next sc. Rep from * around, ending last rep with sl st in first sc of rnd. Fasten off.

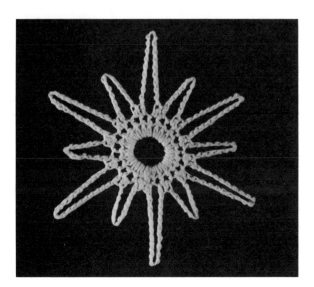

## ◀ Snowflake #13

Approximately 3¼″ diameter

### Materials
DMC Cebelia #20, 18 yds.
Size 10 steel crochet hook.

Ch 10; join with sl st in first ch to form ring.
**Rnd 1:** Work 18 sc in ring; join in first sc.
**Rnd 2:** Sc in same place, [ch 7, skip next 2 sc, sc in next sc] 5 times, ch 7, skip next 2 sc; sl st in first sc of rnd.
**Rnd 3:** In each ch-7 lp, work 2 sc, *ch 4, sl st in 4th ch from hook for picot*, [sc in lp, work picot] 4 times, 2 sc in lp. Join in first sc—6 points.
**Rnd 4:** Sl st in back of this sc and in back of sc of Rnd 2. Holding points forward and working in skipped sts of Rnd 1, [sc in next sc, ch 17, skip next free sc] 6 times; join in first sc of rnd.
**Rnd 5:** In each ch-17 lp, work 8 sc, [work picot, sc in lp] 5 times, work 7 sc in lp. Join in first sc.
**Rnd 6:** Sl st down back of work to Rnd 1. Holding points forward and working in skipped sts of Rnd 1, [sc in next free sc, ch 27] 6 times, sl st in first sc of rnd.
**Rnd 7:** In each ch-27 lp work 14 sc, [work picot, sc in lp] 5 times, work 13 sc in lp. Join in first sc of rnd; fasten off.

## ◀ Snowflake #15

Approximately 3″ diameter

### Materials
DMC Cebelia #10, 4½ yds.
Size 7 steel crochet hook.

Ch 10; join with sl st in first ch to form ring.
**Rnd 1:** Ch 2, work 23 hdc in ring, join in top of beg ch 2.
**Rnd 2:** Ch 1, sc in same sp, ch 12, sc in next sc, ch 20, [sc in next sc, ch 12, sc in next sc, ch 20] 5 times; join in first sc. Fasten off.

## ◄ *Snowflake #16*

Approximately 3¼″ diameter

### *Materials*
DMC Cebelia #10, 17 yds.
Size 7 steel crochet hook.

Ch 7; join with sl st in first ch to form ring.

**Rnd 1:** Work 12 sc in ring; join with sl st in first sc.

**Rnd 2:** Ch 4 (counts as dc and ch 1), [dc in next sc, ch 1] 11 times; join in 3rd ch of beg ch 4.

**Rnd 3:** Sc in same sp, [2 sc in next ch-2 sp, sc in next dc] 11 times, 2 sc in last ch-1 sp, join in first sc.

**Rnd 4:** Ch 3 (counts as dc), dc in next sc, work popcorn over next 2 sts as follows—*[yo and draw up a lp in sp, yo and draw through 2 lps] 3 times,* rep bet *s once in next st, yo and draw through all 7 lps on hook, ch 1,* dc in each of next 2 sc, ch 3, **dc in each of next 2 sc, work popcorn over next 2 sc, dc in each of next 2 sc. Rep from ** 4 times, join in top of beg ch 3.

**Rnd 5:** Ch 3, work popcorn over next dc and popcorn, work popcorn over ch-1 of same popcorn and next dc, dc in next dc, ch 3, 3 sc in ch-3 sp, *dc in next dc, work 2 popcorns as before, dc in next dc; ch 3, 3 sc in ch-3 sp, ch 3. Rep from * 4 times, join in top of beg ch 3.

**Rnd 6:** Ch 3, *dc in top of popcorn, work popcorn over ch-1 of popcorn and top of next popcorn, dc in ch 1 of popcorn, dc in next dc, ch 3, skip ch-3 sp and next sc, sc in next sc, ch 3, skip next sc and ch-3 sp,* [dc in next dc, rep from * to *] 5 times, join in top of beg ch 3.

**Rnd 7:** Ch 2 (counts as hdc), *dc in next st, tr in top of popcorn, ch 1, tr in ch 1 of popcorn, dc in next st, hdc in next st, 3 sc in next ch-3 sp, skip sc, 3 sc in next ch-3 sp, hdc in next dc. Rep from * around, ending last rep with 3 sc in last ch-3 sp, join in top of beg ch 2. Fasten off.

## ◄ *Snowflake #17*

Approximately 5″ diameter

### *Materials*
DMC pearl cotton #5, 18 yds.
Size 4 steel crochet hook.

Ch 10; join with sl st in first ch to form ring.
**Rnd 1:** Work 18 sc in ring; join in first sc.
**Rnd 2:** Sc in same sc, *ch 11, sc in next sc, skip next sc, sc in next sc; rep from * 4 times, ch 11, sc in next sc, skip next sc, sl st in first sc of rnd.
**Rnd 3:** [Work 15 sc in next ch-11 lp, sc bet next 2 sc on ring] 6 times; sl st in first sc of rnd—6 points.
**Rnd 4:** Sl st in each of next 6 sc, *ch 10, skip next 3 sts, sl st in next sc of same lp, skip next 7 sts, sl st in next st of next lp, ch 10, skip next 3 sc, sl st in next st of same lp. Rep from * 5 times.
**Rnd 5:** Work 10 sc in each ch-10 lp, sl st in first sc of rnd.
**Rnd 6:** Sl st in each of next 2 sts, †*[*ch 5, sl st in 5th ch from hook for picot*, sl st in next st] 4 times,* skip next 5 sts, sl st in next st; rep bet *s once, ch 11, sc in 2nd ch from hook and in each of next 9 chs, sl st in same sc of lp, skip 5 sts, sl st in next st. Rep from † 5 times; fasten off.

## *Snowflake #18* ▲

Approximately 5¼″ diameter

### *Materials*
DMC pearl cotton #5, 19½ yds.
Size 4 steel crochet hook.

Ch 10; join with sl st in first ch to form ring.
**Rnd 1:** Ch 3; work 23 dc in ring; join in top of beg ch 3.
**Rnd 2:** Sc in same sp, hdc and dc in next dc, dc and hdc in next dc, sc in next dc, [sc in next dc, hdc and dc in next dc, dc and hdc in next dc, sc in next dc] 5 times; join in first sc—6 points.
**Rnd 3:** Sc in same sp and in next hdc; *hdc in next dc, work dc, tr and dc in sp bet 2 dc of previous rnd; hdc in next hdc, sc in each of next 3 sts. Rep from * 4 times, ending last rep with sc in 2 sts, join in first sc.
**Rnd 4:** Sc in next sc, [ch 12, sc in tr of next point, ch 12, sc in center sc bet points] 5 times, ch 12, sc in tr of next point, ch 6, yo 4 times and draw up a lp in first sc of rnd, [yo and draw through 2 lps] 5 times.
**Rnd 5:** Sc around st just made, [ch 15, sc in next ch-12 lp, ch 7, sc in next ch-12 lp] 5 times, ch 15, sc in next ch-12 lp, ch 7, sc in first sc.
**Rnd 6:** Sc in same st, *ch 9, sl st in 9th ch from hook for large picot, sl st in last sc made, ch 12, dc in next ch-15 lp, work picot, sl st in dc, ch 12, sc in next sc, work picot, sl st in last sc made, ch 9, sc in next sc. Rep from * 5 times, ending last rep with sl st in first sc of rnd. Fasten off.

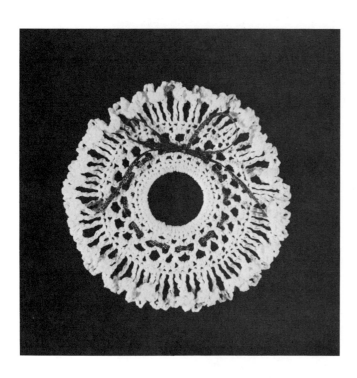

## ◀ *Wreath #1*

Approximately 3″ diameter

### *Materials*
DMC Cebelia #20, 30 yds.
Size 10 steel crochet hook.
13″ Balger ⅛″-wide ribbon.

Ch 30; join with sl st in first ch to form ring.
**Rnd 1:** Ch 2, work 49 hdc in ring; join in top of beg ch 2.
**Rnd 2:** *Sc in next hdc, ch 2, skip next hdc; rep from * around, end with ch 2, join in first sc—25 spaces.
**Rnd 3:** *Sc in next ch-2 sp, ch 4; rep from * around, end with sl st in first sc.
**Rnd 4:** Sl st to center of next ch-4 sp, sc in same sp, *ch 4, sc in next ch-4 sp; rep from * around, ending last rep with sl st in first sc.
**Rnd 5:** Sl st in next ch-4 sp, ch 2, 2 hdc in same sp, 3 hdc in each ch-4 sp around, join in top of beg ch 2—75 hdc.
**Rnd 6:** Ch 9 (counts as tr and ch 4), *tr in next hdc, ch 4; rep from * around, end with sl st in 5th ch of beg ch 9.
**Rnd 7:** Sc in same sp, *ch 3, sc in next ch-4 sp, ch 3, sc in next tr; rep from * around, end last rep with sl st in first sc. Fasten off.

Using a blunt needle, thread ribbon through Rnd 3; tie ends in a bow.

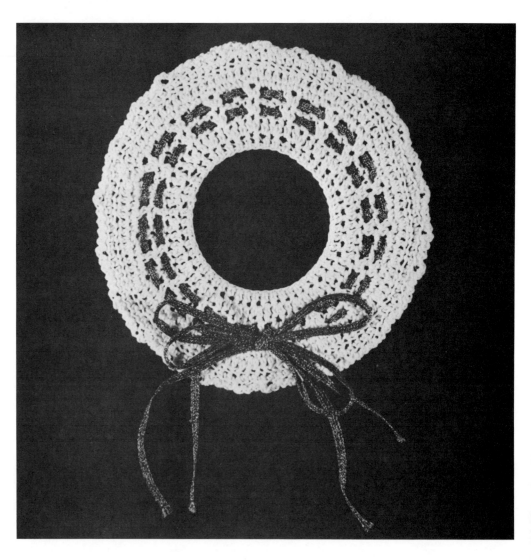

## ◄ *Wreath #2*

Approximately 4¼″ diameter

### *Materials*
DMC Cebelia #10, 28 yds.
Size 7 steel crochet hook.
Balger ⅛-wide ribbon—½ yd. each of two different colors.

Ch 5; join with sl st in first ch to form ring.
**Rnd 1:** Ch 2 (counts as hdc), hdc in each ch around; join in top of beg ch 2—50 hdc.
**Rnd 2:** Ch 2, hdc in same sp, hdc in next hdc, *2 hdc in next hdc, hdc in next hdc; rep from * around; join in top of beg ch 2—75 hdc.
**Rnd 3:** Ch 2, hdc in same sp, ch 1, skip next hdc, *hdc in next hdc, ch 1, skip next hdc, 2 hdc in next hdc, ch 1, skip next hdc; rep from * around; join in top of beg ch 2.
**Rnd 4:** Sl st in sp before next hdc, ch 2, hdc in same sp, ch 1, skip ch-1 sp, hdc in next hdc, ch 1, skip ch-1 sp, *2 hdc bet next 2 hdc, ch 1, skip ch-1 sp, hdc in next hdc, ch 1, skip ch-1 sp. Rep from * around; join in top of beg ch 2.
**Rnd 5:** Ch 1, 2 sc in sp before next hdc, sc in next ch-1 sp, sc in next hdc, sc in next ch-1 sp, *2 sc bet next 2 hdc, sc in next ch-1 sp, sc in next hdc, sc in next ch-1 sp. Rep from * around; join in first sc.
**Rnd 6:** Ch 2, *turn*, hdc in each of next 2 sc, *2 hdc in next sc, hdc in each of next 3 sc; rep from * around; join in top of beg ch 2.
**Rnd 7:** Ch 1, *turn*; working in back lps of sts, sc in each hdc around; join in first sc.
**Rnd 8:** Work sl st and ch 1 in each sc; join. Fasten off.

Thread one ribbon through Rnd 4, over 1 hdc and under 2. Starting at the same place, thread other ribbon through Rnd 3; tie all ends in a bow.

## *Wreath #3* ▲

Approximately 4¾″ diameter

### *Materials*
DMC pearl cotton #5, 19 yds.
Size 4 steel crochet hook.
18″ Balger ⅛″-wide ribbon.

Ch 35; join with sl st in first ch to form ring.
**Rnd 1:** Work 50 sc in ring; join in first sc.
**Rnd 2:** Ch 3, hdc in each of next 3 sc, *work popcorn in next st as follows: [*yo and draw up a lp in st, yo and draw through 2 lps*] 5 times, yo and draw through all 6 lps on hook, ch 1*, hdc in 4 sc. Rep from * 8 times, work popcorn in next sc, join in top of beg ch 3.
**Rnd 3:** Ch 1, sc in same sp, sc in each hdc and popcorn around; join in first sc—50 sc.
**Rnd 4:** Sc in same sc, ch 4, skip next sc, [sc in next sc, ch 4, skip next sc] 23 times, ch 2, dc in first sc to bring thread into position for next rnd.
**Rnd 5:** [Ch 5, sc in next ch-4 lp] 24 times, ch 3, dc in dc of previous rnd.
**Rnd 6:** [Ch 9, sc in next ch-5 lp] 24 times, ch 3, dtr in dc of previous rnd.
**Rnd 7:** Ch 1, *ch 4, *ch 6, sl st in 6th ch from hook for picot*, ch 4, sc in next ch-9 lp; rep from * 24 times, ending last rep with sl st in dtr of previous rnd. Fasten off.

Using a blunt needle, thread ribbon through Rnd 4; tie ends in a bow.

## Ball #1 ▶

Approximately 2″ diameter

### Materials
DMC Cebelia #20, 59 yds.
Size 10 steel crochet hook.

Ch 86.

**Rnd 1:** Tr in 6th ch from hook, ch 2, *tr in next ch, ch 2, tr in same ch, ch 2; rep from * across to last ch, work tr, ch 2 and tr in last ch.

**Rnd 2:** Ch 7, turn, tr in same sp, ch 2, *tr in next tr, ch 2, tr in same tr, ch 2. Rep from * across, ending with tr, ch 2 and tr in 3rd ch of beg ch 5.

**Rnd 3:** Ch 1, turn, sl st in first tr, ch 1, work sl st and ch 1 in each ch-2 sp and tr across, ending with sl st in 5th ch of beg ch-7. Fasten off.

**Rnd 4:** Working on opposite side of starting ch, attach thread in first ch, sc in same sp, *skip 1 ch, sc in next ch. Repeat from * across, ending with sc in last ch.

**Rnd 5:** Ch 1, turn, sc in same sp, *skip next sc, sc in next sc; rep from * across, ending with sc in last sc.

**Rnd 6:** Ch 1, turn, sc in same sp, *skip next 2 sc, sc in next sc; rep from * across, ending with sc in last sc, sl st in first sc of row. Fasten off.

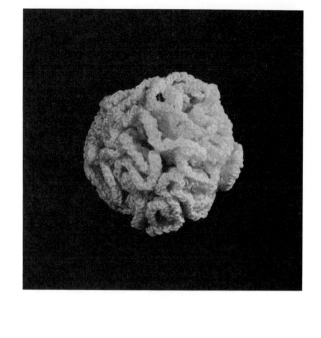

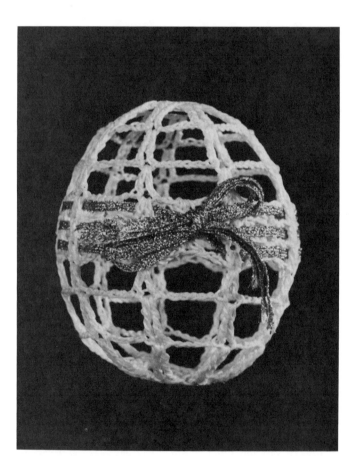

## ◀ Ball #2

Approximately 3¼″ high, 3″ wide

### Materials
DMC pearl cotton #5, 20 yds.
Size 4 steel crochet hook.
1½ yds. Balger ⅛″-wide ribbon.

Ch 10; join with sl st in first ch to form ring.

**Rnd 1:** Work 18 sc in ring; join in first sc of rnd.

**Rnd 2:** Ch 5 (counts as dtr), dtr in each of next 2 sc, [ch 5, dtr in next sc] 8 times, ch 5, join in top of beg ch 5.

**Rnd 3:** Sl st in sp before next dtr, ch 4 (counts as tr), tr in same sp, [ch 5, skip next ch-5 sp, 2 tr bet next 2 dtr] 8 times, ch 5, join in top of beg ch 4.

**Rnd 4:** Sl st in sp before next tr, ch 3 (counts as dc), dc in same sp, [ch 6, skip ch-5 sp, 2 dc bet next 2 tr] 8 times, ch 6, join in top of beg ch 3.

**Rnd 5:** Sl st in sp before next dc, ch 2 (counts as hdc), hdc in same sp, [ch 3, 2 hdc in next ch-6 sp, ch 3, 2 hdc bet next 2 dc] 8 times, ch 3, 2 hdc in next ch-6 sp, ch 3; join in top of beg ch 2.

**Rnds 6 & 7:** Sl st in sp before next hdc, ch 2, hdc in same sp, [ch 3, skip ch-3 sp, hdc bet next 2 hdc] 17 times, ch 3; join in top of beg ch 2.

**Rnd 8:** Sl st in sp before next hdc, ch 3, dc in same sp, [ch 6, skip next ch-3 sp, 2 hdc and ch-3 sp, 2 hdc bet next 2 hdc] 8 times, ch 6, skip next ch-3 sp, 2 hdc and ch-3 sp; join in top of beg ch 3.

**Rnd 9:** Sl st in sp before next dc, ch 4, tr in same sp, [ch 5, skip ch-6 sp, 2 tr bet next 2 dc] 8 times, ch 5; join in top of beg ch 4.

**Rnd 10:** Sl st in sp before next tr, ch 5, dtr in same sp, [ch 1, skip ch-5 sp, 2 dtr bet next 2 tr] 8 times, ch 1; join in top of beg ch 5.

**Rnd 11:** Sc in sp before next dtr, sc in next ch-1 sp, [sc bet next 2 dtr, sc in ch-1 sp] 8 times, join in first sc.

**Rnd 12:** Sl st in each st around, fasten off.

Starch and shape ball into an oval. Cut ribbon into three 18″ strands. Thread a strand through Rnds 5, 6 and 7. Make a single bow with all three strands.

## Ball #3 ▶

Approximately 1½″ diameter

### Materials
DMC Cebelia #20, 22 yds.
Size 10 steel crochet hook.

Ch 69 loosely.
**Row 1:** Sc in 9th ch from hook, *ch 7, sc in next ch; rep from * across.
**Row 2:** Ch 1, turn, sl st in 3 chs of last ch 7 of previous row, sc in same ch-7 lp, ch 12, sc in same lp, *ch 12, sc in next ch-7 lp, ch 12, sc in same lp; rep from * across.
**Row 3:** Ch 1, turn, sl st in 3 chs of first ch-lp of Row 1; working on opposite side of starting ch, sc in first ch, *skip next 2 chs, sc in next ch. Rep from * across, ending with an sc in last ch.
**Row 4:** Ch 1, turn, sc in first sc, *skip next 2 sc, sc in next sc; rep from * across, end with sc in last sc. Sl st in first sc of row to form a circle. Fasten off.

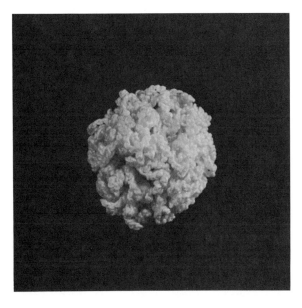

## ◀ Ball #4

Approximately 2¾″ diameter

### Materials
DMC pearl cotton #5, 18 yds.
Size 4 steel crochet hook.
Balger's ⅛″-wide ribbon—1 yd. each of two different colors.

Ch 10; join with sl st in first ch to form ring.
**Rnd 1:** Ch 3 (counts as dc), dc in ring, ch 2, [2 dc in ring, ch 2] 7 times; join in top of beg ch 3.
**Rnd 2:** Ch 3, dc in next dc, ch 3, [dc in each of next 2 dc, ch 3] 7 times, join in top of beg ch 3.
**Rnd 3:** Sc in sp before next dc, ch 7, sc in 2nd ch from hook and in each of next 5 chs, sc in same sp on ring, sc in next ch-3 sp, [sc bet next 2 dc, ch 7, sc in 2nd ch from hook and in each of next 5 chs, sc bet same 2 dc of ring, 3 sc in next ch-3 sp] 7 times; join in first sc of rnd—8 points. Fasten off.
**Rnd 4:** With right side facing, attach thread in tip of any point, sc in same point, ch 9, [sc in tip of next point, ch 9] 7 times; join in first sc of rnd.
**Rnd 5:** Sc in same sp, [ch 4, sc in ch-9 sp] twice, ch 4, *sc in next sc, [ch 4, sc in ch-9 sp] twice, ch 4. Rep from * 6 times; join in first sc of rnd.
**Rnd 6:** Sl st in first 2 chs of first ch-4 sp, sc in same ch-4 sp, ch 4, [sc in next ch-4 sp, ch 4] 23 times; join in first sc of rnd.
**Rnd 7:** *3 sc in each of next 2 ch-4 sps, sc in next ch-4 sp, ch 7, sc in 2nd ch from hook and in each of next 5 chs, sc in same ch-4 sp; rep from * 7 times, join in first sc. Fasten off.
**Rnd 8:** With right side facing, attach thread in tip of any point, sc in same point, ch 3, [sc in tip of next point, ch 3] 7 times, join in first sc.
**Rnd 9:** Sc in same sc, 3 sc in next ch-3 sp, [sc in next sc, 3 sc in next ch-3 sp] 7 times, join in first sc.
**Rnd 10:** Ch 3, dc in same sp, ch 1, skip next 3 sc, [2 dc in next sc, ch 1, skip next 3 sc] 7 times, join in top of beg ch 3.
**Rnd 11:** Sl st in next dc and in ch-1 sp, ch 2, [2 hdc in next ch-1 sp] 7 times; join in top of beg ch 2.
**Rnd 12:** Sl st in every other st around; join and fasten off.

Cut ribbon into 12″ lengths. Pull all six lengths through sps directly opposite one another on Rnd 1. Tie and knot and leave ends free.

## Ball #6 ▼

Approximately 3″ diameter

### Materials
DMC Cebelia #10, 21 yds.
Size 7 steel crochet hook.
24″ Balger ⅛″-wide ribbon.

Ch 6; join with sl st in first ch to form ring.
**Rnd 1:** Work 12 sc in ring; join in first sc.
**Rnd 2:** Ch 3 (counts as dc), [2 dc in next dc, dc in next dc] 5 times, 2 dc in next dc; join in top of beg ch 3—18 dc.
**Rnd 3:** Ch 4 (counts as dc and ch 1), [dc in next dc, ch 1] 17 times; join in 3rd ch of beg ch 4.
**Rnd 4:** Ch 5, [dc in next dc, ch 2] 17 times; join in 3rd ch of beg ch 5.
**Rnd 5:** Ch 7, [dc in next dc, ch 4] 17 times; join in 3rd ch of beg ch 7.
**Rnd 6:** Ch 9, [tr in next dc, ch 5] 17 times; join in 4th ch of beg ch 9.
**Rnds 7 & 8:** Ch 10, [dtr in next st, ch 5] 17 times; join in 5th ch of beg ch 10.
**Rnd 9:** Ch 8, [dtr in next dtr, ch 3] 17 times; join in 5th ch of beg ch 8.
**Rnd 10:** Ch 6, [tr in next dtr, ch 2] 17 times; join in 4th ch of beg ch 6.
**Rnd 11:** Ch 4, [dc in next tr, ch 1] 17 times; join in 3rd ch of beg ch 4.
**Rnd 12:** [Sl st in next ch-1 sp] 18 times; join in first sl st. Fasten off.

Starch and shape ball. Cut ribbon in half. Thread strands through Rnds 3 and 4 and tie ends in a bow.

## Ball #5 ▲

Approximately 4″ high, 3¼″ wide

### Materials
DMC pearl cotton #5, 13 yds.
Size 4 steel crochet hook.
12″ Balger ⅛″-wide ribbon.

Ch 12; join with sl st in first ch to form ring.
**Rnd 1:** [Sc in ring, ch 9] 7 times; ch 4, tr in first sc to bring thread into position for next rnd.
**Rnd 2:** Sc around tr just made, [ch 12, sc in next ch-9 lp] 7 times, ch 6, dtr in first sc of rnd.
**Rnd 3:** Sc around st just made, [ch 15, sc in next ch-lp] 7 times, ch 7, yo hook 4 times, draw up a lp in first sc of rnd, [yo and draw through 2 lps] 5 times.
**Rnd 4:** Sc around st just made, [ch 19, sc in next ch-lp] 7 times, ch 9, yo hook 6 times, draw up a lp in first sc of rnd, [yo and draw through 2 lps] 7 times.
**Rnd 5:** Sc around st just made, [ch 23, sc in next ch-lp] 7 times, ch 11, yo hook 7 times, draw up a lp in first sc of rnd, [yo and draw through 2 lps] 8 times.
**Rnd 6:** Sc around st just made, [ch 19, sc in next ch-lp] 7 times, ch 9, yo hook 6 times, draw up a lp in first sc of rnd, [yo and draw through 2 lps] 7 times.
**Rnd 7:** Sc around st just made, [ch 15, sc in next ch-lp] 7 times, ch 7, yo hook 4 times, draw up a lp in first sc of rnd, [yo and draw through 2 lps] 5 times.
**Rnd 8:** Sc around st just made, [ch 12, sc in next ch-lp] 7 times, ch 6, dtr in first sc of rnd.
**Rnd 9:** Sc around st just made, [ch 9, sc in next ch-lp] 7 times, ch 4, tr in first sc of rnd.
**Rnd 10:** Sc around tr just made, ch 1, [sc in next ch-lp, ch 1] 7 times; join in first sc. Fasten off.

Starch and shape ball into an oval. Tie ribbon to top for hanger.

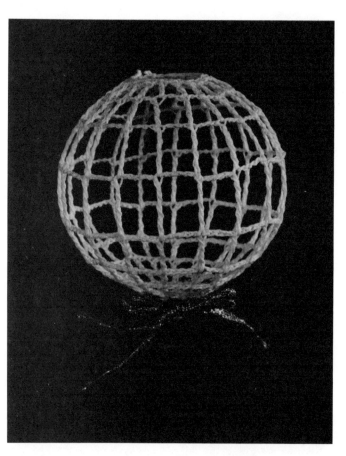

## Ball #7 ▲

Approximately 3″ diameter

### Materials
DMC pearl cotton #5, 27½ yds.
Size 4 steel crochet hook.
60″ Balger ⅛″-wide ribbon.

Ch 12; join with sl st in first ch to form ring.
**Rnd 1:** Ch 3 (counts as dc), dc in ring, ch 2, [2 dc in ring, ch 2] 9 times, join in top of beg ch 3.
**Rnd 2:** Sl st to ch-2 sp, ch 3, dc in same ch-2 sp, ch 3, [2 dc in next ch-2 sp, ch 3] 9 times; join in top of beg ch 3.
**Rnd 3:** Sl st to center of ch-3 sp, ch 3, dc in ch-3 sp, ch 5, [2 dc in ch-3 sp, ch 5] 9 times, join in top of beg ch 3.
**Rnd 4:** Sl st in next dc, [work sc, hdc, dc, tr, dc, hdc and sc in next ch-5 sp, ch 1] 10 times, join in first sc—10 points.

**Rnd 5:** Sl st in next 3 sts, ch 3, dc in same sp, ch 9, [work 2 dc in tr of next point, ch 9] 9 times, join in top of beg ch 3.
**Rnd 6:** Sl st in next dc, [work 2 sc, 2 hdc, dc, tr, dc, 2 hdc, 2 sc and ch 2 in next ch-9 sp] 10 times; join in first sc.
**Rnd 7:** Sl st in next 5 sts, ch 3, dc in same sp, ch 7, [work 2 dc in tr of next point, ch 7] 9 times, join in first sc.
**Rnd 8:** Sl st in next dc, [work 2 sc, hdc, dc, tr, dc, hdc and 2 sc in next ch-7 sp, ch 1] 10 times, join in first sc.
**Rnd 9:** Sl st in next 3 sts, ch 3, dc in same sp, ch 3, [2 dc in tr of next point, ch 3] 9 times, join in top of beg ch 3.
**Rnd 10:** Sl st in next dc and in ch-3 sp, ch 3, dc in same sp, ch 1, [2 dc in next ch-3 sp, ch 1] 9 times, join in top of beg ch 3.
**Rnd 11:** Sl st in next dc and in ch-1 sp, ch 3, dc in same sp, 2 dc in each ch-1 sp around, join in top of beg ch 3.
**Rnd 12:** Sl st in each st around. Fasten off.

Cut ribbon into five 12″ strands. Tie a strand around every other 2-dc group of Rnd 1.

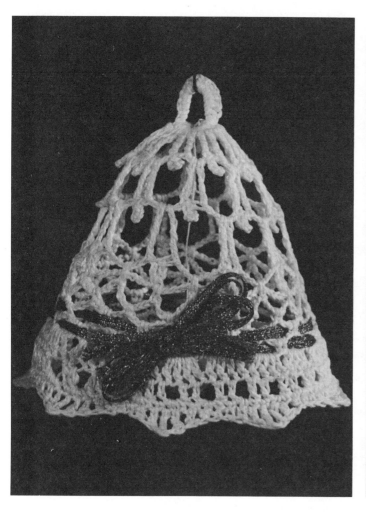

## ▲ *Bell #1*

Approximately 4¼″ diameter; 4¼″ high

### *Materials*
DMC pearl cotton #5, 41 yds.
Size 4 steel crochet hook.
30″ Balger ⅛″-wide ribbon.
Small amount polyester stuffing.

Ch 10; join with sl st in first ch to form ring.
**Rnd 1:** Work 20 sc in ring; join in first sc.
**Rnd 2:** Ch 5 (counts as dtr), *ch 6, sl st in 6th ch from hook for picot*, sl st in top of beg ch 5, dtr in next sc, [ch 3, dtr in next sc, work picot, sl st in last dtr made, dtr in next sc] 9 times, ch 1, hdc in top of beg ch 5 to bring thread into position for next rnd.
**Rnd 3:** Ch 5, work picot, sl st in top of beg ch 5, dtr around hdc at end of last rnd, [ch 5, dtr in next ch-3 sp, work picot, sl st in last dtr made, dtr in same ch-3 sp] 9 times, ch 2, dc in top of beg ch 5.
**Rnd 4:** Ch 5, work picot, sl st in top of beg ch 5, dtr around dc at end of last rnd, ch 7, [dtr in next ch-5 sp, work picot, sl st in last dtr made, dtr in same ch-5 sp] 9 times, ch 7; join in top of beg ch 5.
**Rnd 5:** Sl st to top of first picot, sc in same picot, ch 9, [sc in next picot, ch 9] 9 times; join in first sc.
**Rnd 6:** Sc in same sp, [ch 7, work sc over ch 9 and ch 7 of Rnds 5 & 4, ch 7, sc in next sc] 9 times, ch 7, work sc over ch 9 and ch 7 of Rnds 5 & 4, ch 2, tr in first sc of rnd.
**Rnds 7 & 8:** Sc around st just made, [ch 5, sc in next ch-7 sp] 19 times, ch 2, dc in first sc of rnd.

**Rnd 9:** Sc around dc just made, ch 5, [sc in next ch-5 sp, ch 5] 19 times; join in first sc of rnd.
**Rnd 10:** Sl st in next ch-5 sp, ch 3, work 4 dc in each ch-5 sp around; join in top of beg ch 3—81 dc.
**Rnd 11:** Ch 3, dc in next dc, ch 1, skip next dc, *dc in each of next 2 dc, ch 1, skip next dc; rep from * around; join in top of beg ch 3.
**Rnd 12:** Sc in sp before next dc, 2 sc in ch-1 sp, *sc bet next 2 sc, 2 sc in next ch-1 sp; rep from * around, join in first sc.
**Rnd 13:** [Sc in next st, hdc in next st, dc in next st, tr in each of next 2 sts, dc in next st, hdc in next st, sc in next st] 8 times; join in first sc. Fasten off.

For handle, join thread to any sc of Rnd 1, ch 9, sl st in st on opposite side of rnd. Turn and sc in each ch; sl st in base of ch. Fasten off.

### *Clapper*
Ch 5; join with sl st in first ch to form ring.
**Rnd 1:** Work 9 sc in ring; join in first sc.
**Rnd 2:** Ch 2 (counts as hdc), [2 hdc in next sc, hdc in next hdc] 4 times; join in top of beg ch 3—13 hdc.
**Rnd 3:** Ch 3 (counts as dc), [2 dc in next hdc, dc in next hdc] 6 times; join in top of beg ch 3—19 dc.
**Rnd 4:** Ch 3, dc in each dc around; join in top of beg ch 3.
**Rnd 5:** Ch 2, [skip next hdc, hdc in each of next 2 hdc] 6 times; join in top of beg ch 2. Stuff.
**Rnd 6:** [Sc in next hdc, skip next hdc] 6 times; join in first sc and close opening. Fasten off, leaving several inches of thread for attaching. Tie clapper inside bell.

Cut ribbon in half. Thread strands through Rnds 8 and 9 and tie ends in a bow.

## ◄ Bell #2

Approximately 2¾″ diameter, 3¾″ high

**Materials**
DMC Cebelia #10, 49 yds.
Size 7 steel crochet hook.
30″ Balger ⅛″-wide ribbon.
Small amount polyester stuffing.

Ch 10; join with sl st in first ch to form ring.
**Rnd 1:** Ch 2 (counts as hdc), work 29 hdc in ring; join in top of beg ch 2—30 hdc.
**Rnd 2:** Ch 6 (counts as dc and ch 3), [skip 2 hdc, dc in next hdc, ch 3] 9 times; join in 3rd ch of beg ch 6.
**Rnd 3:** Ch 8, [dc in next dc, ch 5] 9 times; join in 3rd ch of beg ch 8.
**Rnd 4:** Ch 5 (counts as hdc and ch 3), hdc in next ch-5 sp, [ch 3, hdc in next dc, ch 3, hdc in next ch-5 sp] 9 times, ch 3; join in 2nd ch of beg ch 5.
**Rnd 5:** Sl st in next ch-3 sp, ch 3 (counts as dc), dc in same sp; 2 dc in each ch-3 sp around; join in top of beg ch 3—20 dc.
**Rnd 6:** Ch 2 (counts as hdc), hdc in same sp, [ch 1, skip next dc, 2 hdc in next hdc] 19 times, ch 1, skip next dc; join in top of beg ch 2.
**Rnd 7:** Sl st in sp before next hdc, *ch 2, *ch 5, sl st in 5th ch from hook for small picot*, ch 2, skip ch-1 sp, sl st bet next 2 hdc. Rep from * 18 times, ch 2, hdc in sl st at base of first ch 2 of rnd, ch 3, hdc in hdc just made.
**Rnd 8:** Ch 2 (counts as hdc), 2 hdc in same sp, [ch 2, work small picot, ch 2, 3 hdc in next picot] 19 times, ch 2, hdc in top of beg ch 2, ch 3, hdc in hdc just made.
**Rnd 9:** [Ch 4, sl st in next picot] 19 times, ch 4, sl st in first picot.
**Rnd 10:** Sl st in next ch-4 sp, ch 3 (counts as dc), 2 dc in same sp, 3 dc in each ch-4 sp around, join in top of beg ch 3—60 dc.
**Rnd 11:** Ch 3, dc in each dc around; join in top of beg ch-3.
**Rnd 12:** Sc in same sp, sc in each of next 2 dc, *ch 7, sl st in 7th ch from hook for large picot*, sl st in dc just worked in, sc in each of next 3 dc. Rep from * 18 times, work large picot, sl st in dc just worked in, sl st in first sc of rnd. Fasten off.

For handle, attach thread to any hdc of Rnd 1, ch 9, sl st in hdc on opposite side of ring; turn, work 12 sc over ch 9. Sl st in base of ch. Fasten off.

**Clapper**
Ch 5; join with sl st in first ch to form ring.
**Rnd 1:** Ch 2, work 9 hdc in ring; join in top of beg ch 2.
**Rnd 2:** Sc in same sp, 2 sc in next hdc, [sc in next hdc, 2 sc in next hdc] 4 times; join in first sc—15 sc.
**Rnd 3:** Ch 2, hdc in same sp, hdc in next sc, [2 hdc in next sc, sc in next sc] 6 times, 2 hdc in next hdc; join to top of beg ch 2—23 hdc.
**Rnds 4–8:** Ch 2, hdc in each hdc around; join in top of beg ch 2. Stuff clapper.
**Rnd 9:** [Sc in next sc, skip next sc] 11 times; *do not join.*
**Rnd 10:** Sl st in next st, skip next st; rep from * around until opening is closed. Fasten off, leaving a long thread. Tie clapper inside bell.

Cut ribbon into a 12″ and an 18″ strand. Thread shorter strand through Rnd 5; tie ends in a bow. Thread remaining strand through Rnd 10; tie ends in a bow.

## ▲ Bell #3

Approximately 3⅛″ diameter, 3″ high

**Materials**
DMC pearl cotton #5, 21 yds.
Size 4 steel crochet hook.
12″ Balger ⅛″-wide ribbon.
Small amount polyester stuffing.

Ch 5; join with sl st in first ch to form ring.
**Rnd 1:** Work 10 sc in ring; join in first sc.
**Rnd 2:** Ch 3 (counts as dc), [2 dc in next sc, dc in next sc] 4 times, 2 dc in last sc; join in top of beg ch 3—15 dc.
**Rnds 3 & 4:** Ch 4 (counts as dc and ch 1), [dc in next dc, ch 1] 14 times, join in 3rd ch of beg ch 4.
**Rnds 5 & 6:** Ch 5, [dc in next dc, ch 2] 14 times; join in 3rd ch of beg ch 5.
**Rnds 7 & 8:** Ch 6, [dc in next dc, ch 3] 14 times; join in 3rd ch of beg ch 6.
**Rnd 9:** Ch 7, [dc in next dc, ch 4] 14 times, join in 3rd ch of beg ch 7.
**Rnd 10:** Ch 8, [dc in next dc, ch 5] 14 times, join in 3rd ch of beg ch 8.
**Rnd 11:** Work [sc, hdc, 2 dc, hdc and sc] in each ch-5 sp across; join in first sc. Fasten off.

For handle, attach thread to any st of Rnd 1, ch 9, sl st in st on opposite side of ring, turn, work 12 sc over ch 9. Sl st in base of ch. Fasten off.

**Clapper**
Ch 5; join with sl st in first ch to form ring.
**Rnd 1:** Ch 3, work 9 dc in ring; join in top of beg ch 3.
**Rnd 2:** Ch 3, [2 dc in next dc, dc in next dc] 4 times, 2 dc in next dc; join in top of beg ch 3—15 dc.
**Rnd 3:** Ch 2, hdc in next st, skip next st, [hdc in each of next 2 sts, skip next st] 4 times; join in top of beg ch 2. Stuff.
**Rnd 4:** [Sc in next sc, skip next sc] 5 times. Fasten off. Close opening, leaving several inches of thread for tying. Tie clapper inside bell.

Thread ribbon through Rnd 4 and tie ends in a bow.

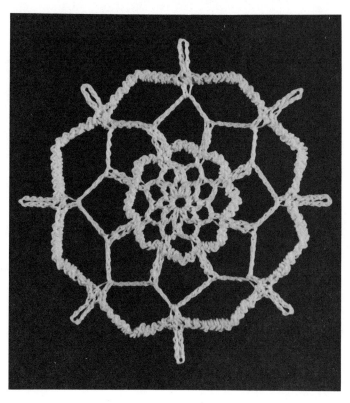

## ◀ *Star #1*

Approximately 4″ diameter

### *Materials*
DMC Cebelia #10, 11 yds.
Size 7 steel crochet hook.

Ch 6; join with sl st in first ch to form ring.
**Rnd 1:** [Sc in ring, ch 3] 7 times; sc in ring, ch 2, hdc in first sc to bring thread into position for next row.
**Rnd 2:** Sc around hdc just made, [ch 4, sc in next ch-3 sp] 7 times, ch 2, dc in first sc of rnd.
**Rnd 3:** Sc around dc just made, [ch 6, sc in next ch-4 sp] 7 times, ch 6, sl st in first sc of rnd.
**Rnd 4:** Sc in same sp, *ch 6, sl st in 6th ch from hook for picot*, sc in last sc worked in, *[sl st, ch 1] 5 times in next ch-6 sp, work sc, picot and sc in next sc. Rep from * 6 times, work [sl st, ch 1] 5 times in next ch-6 sp; join in first st of rnd.
**Rnd 5:** Sl st to top of picot, [sc in picot, ch 10] 7 times, ch 5, dtr in first sc of rnd.
**Rnd 6:** Sc around dtr just made, [ch 15, sc in next ch-10 sp] 7 times, ch 15, sl st in first sc of rnd.
**Rnd 7:** Sc in same sp, *ch 9, sl st in 9th ch from hook for large picot*, sc in same sc, *[sl st in ch-15 sp, ch 1] 8 times, work sc, large picot and sc in next sc. Rep from * 6 times, [sl st in ch-15 sp, ch 1] 8 times, sl st in first sc of rnd. Fasten off.

## *Star #2* ▶

Approximately 4″ diameter

### *Materials*
DMC Cebelia #10, 13 yds.
Size 7 steel crochet hook.

Ch 12; join with sl st in first ch to form ring.
**Rnd 1:** Work 25 sc in ring; join with sl st in first sc.
**Rnd 2:** *Ch 15, skip next 3 sc, sl st in each of next 2 sc. Rep from * 4 times, ending last rep with sl st in joining sl st of previous rnd.
**Rnd 3:** *Work 4 sc, 3 hdc, 2 dc, 2 tr, 2 dc, 3 hdc and 4 sc in next ch-15 lp, sl st in next sl st. Rep from * 4 times—5 points.
**Rnd 4:** *[Sl st in next sc of point, ch 1] twice, sl st in next sc, *ch 4, sl st in 4th ch from hook for picot*, [sl st in next st, ch 1, sl st in next st, work picot] twice, [sl st in next st, ch 1] twice, sl st bet 2 tr at tip of point, [ch 1, work picot] 7 times, ch 1, sl st bet same 2 tr of point, skip second tr of point, [ch 1, sl st in next st] twice, work picot, [sl st in next st, ch 1, sl st in next st, work picot] twice, [sl st in next st, ch 1] twice, sl st in last sc of point. Rep from * 4 times, sl st in first sl st of rnd. Fasten off.

## Star #3  ▶

Approximately 1¾″ diameter

### Materials
DMC Cebelia #20, 4 yds.
Size 10 steel crochet hook.

Ch 7; join with sl st in first ch to form ring.
**Rnd 1:** Ch 2, work 17 hdc in ring; join in top of beg ch 2.
**Rnd 2:** Ch 3 (counts as dc), dc in next st, ch 3, [dc in each of next 2 sts, ch 3] 8 times, join in top of beg ch 3.
**Rnd 3:** (*Ch 6, sl st in 6th ch from hook for picot*) 3 times, sl st in top of next dc, 3 sc in next ch-3 sp, sl st in next dc; rep from * 9 times, ending last rep with sl st in joining of last rnd. Fasten off.

## Star #4  ▲

Approximately 4½″ diameter

### Materials
DMC Cebelia #10, 18 yds.
Size 7 steel crochet hook.

Ch 25; join with sl st in first ch to form ring.
**Rnd 1:** *Ch 3, 2 dc in same ch as sl st, skip next 3 chs, 2 dc in next ch, ch 3, sl st in same ch, sl st in next ch; rep from * 4 times—5 points.
**Rnd 2:** Sl st to top of next ch 3, *ch 5, tr in sp bet the 2 groups of dc of point, ch 5, sl st in top of last ch 3 of point, ch 3, sl st in top of first ch 3 of next point. Rep from * 4 times.
**Rnd 3:** Sc in same sp as last sl st, *[ch 3, sc in ch-5 sp] twice, ch 3, sc in tr, [ch 3, sc in ch-5 sp] twice, ch 3, sc in next sl st, ch 3, sc in next sl st. Rep from * 4 times, ending last rep ch 3, sl st in first sc of rnd.

**Rnd 4:** Sl st in first ch of ch-3 sp, sc in same ch-3 sp, *[ch 3, sc in next ch-3 sp] 5 times, ch 3, skip next ch-3 sp, sc in next ch-3 sp. Rep from * 4 times, ending last rep with ch 3, skip next ch-3 sp, sl st in first sc of rnd.
**Rnd 5:** Sl st in first ch of next ch-3 sp, sc in same ch-3 sp, *[ch 3, sc in next ch-3 sp] 4 times, ch 4, skip next ch-3 sp, sc in next ch-3 sp. Rep from * 4 times, ending last rep with ch 4, skip next ch-3 sp, sl st in first sc of rnd.
**Rnd 6:** Sl st in first ch of next ch-3 sp, sc in same ch-3 sp, [ch 3, sc in next ch-3 sp] 3 times, ch 3, 4 sc in ch-4 sp, ch 3, *[sc in next ch-3 sp, ch 3] 4 times, 4 sc in ch-4 sp, ch 3. Rep from * 3 times, sl st in first sc of rnd.
**Rnd 7:** *Sc in next ch-3 sp, *ch 5, sl st in 5th ch from hook for picot*, sc in same ch-3 sp, sc in next ch-3 sp, work 4 picots, sl st in back of 2nd picot, work 1 more picot, sl st in back of 1st picot, sc in same ch-3 sp, work sc, picot and sc in next ch-3 sp, 3 sc in next ch-3 sp, sc in each of next 4 sc, 3 sc in next ch-3 sp. Rep from * 4 times. Fasten off.

*Star #5*

*Star #6*

## ◀ Star #5

Approximately 4¼″ diameter

**Materials**
DMC Cebelia #10, 17 yds.
Size 7 steel crochet hook.

Ch 12; join with sl st in first sc to form ring.
**Rnd 1:** Ch 4, work 29 tr in ring; join in top of beg ch 4.
**Rnd 2:** Ch 1, sc in same sp, ch 2, sc in next tr, *ch 6, sl st in 6th ch from hook for large picot,* *sc in next tr, ch 2, sc in next tr, work picot. Rep from * 13 times, sl st in first sc of rnd.
**Rnd 3:** Ch 1, *sc in next ch-2 sp, ch 10, skip picot; rep from * 13 times, ch 5, skip picot, dtr in first sc of rnd.
**Rnd 4:** Ch 1, sc around dtr just made, *ch 6, sc in next ch-10 lp. Rep from * 13 times, ch 6, sl st in first sc.
**Rnd 5:** *Ch 9, sl st in next sc, ch 4, tr in same sc, work picot, tr in same sc, ch 4, sl st in same sc. Rep from * 14 times. Fasten off.

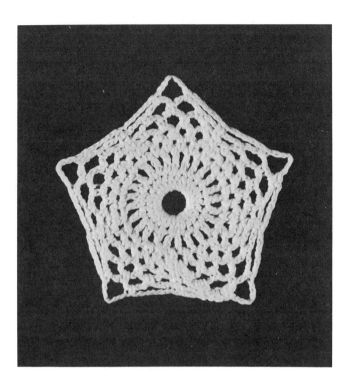

## ◀ Star #6

Approximately 5½″ diameter

**Materials**
DMC pearl cotton #5, 18½ yds.
Size 4 steel crochet hook.

Ch 9; join with sl st in first ch to form ring.
**Rnd 1:** Ch 2, work 19 hdc in ring; join in top of beg ch 2.
**Rnd 2:** Sc in same sp, *ch 21, sc in 2nd ch from hook and in each remaining ch, sc in side of sc at base of ch, sc in each of next 4 sc; rep from * 4 times, ending last rep with sc in each of next 3 sc, join in first sc.
**Rnd 3:** *Working on opposite side of ch of next point, [sc in 2 chs, ch 5, sl st in 5th ch from hook for picot] 9 times, sc in next sc, in tip of point work sc, picot and sc; sc in next sc, [work picot, sc in 2 sc] 9 times, skip next sc, [sc in next sc, skip next sc] twice. Rep from * 4 times; join in first sc. Fasten off.

## Star #7 ▲

Approximately 3″ diameter

**Materials**
DMC pearl cotton #5, 11 yds.
Size 4 steel crochet hook.

Ch 10; join with sl st in first ch to form ring.
**Rnd 1:** Ch 2, work 24 hdc in ring; join in top of beg ch 2.
**Rnd 2:** Ch 4 (counts as dc and ch 1), *dc in next hdc, ch 1; rep from * around; join in 3rd ch of beg ch 4.
**Rnd 3:** *Sc in next ch-1 sp, ch 1; rep from * around; join in first sc.
**Rnd 4:** Sc in same sp as sl st, *[sc in next ch-1 sp, ch 3] 4 times, sc in next ch-1 sp, sc in next sc. Rep from * around, ending last rep with sl st in first sc—5 points.
**Rnd 5:** Sl st in next sc and in ch-3 sp; sc in same ch-3 sp, ch 4, [sc in next ch-3 sp, ch 4] twice, sc in next ch-3 sp, ch 1, skip next sc, sc in next sc, ch 1, *[sc in next ch-3 sp, ch 4] 3 times, sc in next ch-3 sp, ch 1, skip next sc, sc in next sc, ch 1. Rep from * 3 times, ending last rep with sc in joining sl st of last rnd, join in first sc of rnd.
**Rnd 6:** Sl st in each of first 2 chs of ch-4 sp, sc in same ch-4 sp, [ch 5, sc in next ch-4 sp] twice, ch 3, sc in sc bet points, ch 3, *[sc in next ch-4 sp, ch 5] twice, sc in next ch-4 sp, ch 3, sc in sc bet points, ch 3. Rep from * 3 times, join in first sc.
**Rnd 7:** Sl st in each of first 2 chs of ch-5 sp, sc in same ch-5 sp, ch 6, sc in next ch-5 sp, ch 6, skip ch-3 sp, sc in sc bet points, ch 6, skip ch-3 sp, *[sc in next ch-5 sp, ch 6] twice, skip ch-3 sp, sc in sc bet points, ch 6, skip ch-3 sp. Rep from * 3 times, join in first sc. Fasten off.

### ◄ *Star #8*

Approximately 1½″ diameter

**Materials**
DMC Cebelia #20, 3 yds.
Size 10 steel crochet hook.

Ch 5; join with sl st in first ch to form ring.
**Rnd 1:** Work 15 sc in ring; join in first sc.
**Rnd 2:** ★Ch 4, tr in same sp, *ch 6, sl st in 6th ch from hook for picot*, sl st in tr just made, skip next sc, tr in next sc, ch 4, sl st in same sc, work picot and sc in next sc. Rep from ★ around, ending last rep with sl st in joining sl st of previous rnd. Fasten off.

### *Star #9* ►

Approximately 2¼″ diameter

**Materials**
DMC Cebelia #20, 6 yds.
Size 10 steel crochet hook.

Ch 7; join with sl st in first ch to form ring.
**Rnd 1:** Work 15 sc in ring; join in first sc.
**Rnd 2:** Sc in same sp as sl st, ch 20, skip next sc, sc in next sc, [sc in next sc, ch 20, skip next sc, sc in next sc] 4 times; sl st in first sc.
**Rnd 3:** ★Sc in each of 7 chs of next ch-20 lp, hdc in each of next 2 chs, dc and tr in next ch, tr and dc in next ch, hdc in each of next 2 chs, sc in each of next 7 chs, skip first sc bet lps, sc in next sc. Rep from ★ 4 times, ending last rep with sc in joining sl st of previous rnd.
**Rnd 4:** Sl st in each of 18 sts of first point, sl st in 4th st of next point, [sl st in each of next 15 sts, sl st in 4th st of next point] 4 times. Fasten off.

### ◄ *Star #10*

Approximately 2½″ diameter

**Materials**
DMC Cebelia #20, 8 yds.
Size 10 steel crochet hook.

Ch 7; join with sl st in first ch to form ring.
**Rnd 1:** Ch 2, work 14 hdc in ring; join in top of beg ch 2.
**Rnd 2:** Ch 3 (counts as dc); in same sp, [*yo, draw up a lp, yo and draw through 2 lps*] *twice, yo and draw through all 3 lps on hook—starting cluster made,* ch 1, ★in next hdc, [*yo, draw up a lp, yo and draw through 2 lps*] *3 times, yo and draw through all 4 lps on hook—cluster made,* ch 1. Rep from ★ around, join in top of starting cluster.
**Rnd 3:** Working in front lps of sts, work sc, hdc, dc, hdc and sc in top of starting cluster, skip ch-1 sp, ★work sc, hdc, dc, hdc and sc in top of next cluster, skip ch-1 sp. Rep from ★ around, sl st in *back* lp of starting cluster.
**Rnd 4:** Working in back lps of Rnd 2 sts, ★ch 5, dc in next cluster, [*ch 6, sl st in 6th ch from hook for large picot*] 5 times, sl st in dc just made, ch 5, sl st in next cluster, ch 2, sl st in next cluster. Fasten off.

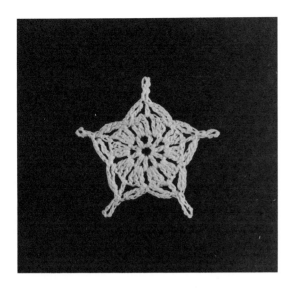

## ◄ *Star #11*

Approximately 1¾″ diameter

### *Materials*
DMC Cebelia #20, 5 yds.
Size 10 steel crochet hook.

Ch 6; join with sl st in first ch to form ring.
**Rnd 1:** Ch 3 (counts as hdc and ch 1), [hdc in ring, ch 1] 9 times; join in 2nd ch of beg ch 3.
**Rnd 2:** Sl st in next ch-1 sp, ch 3 (counts as dc), 2 dc in same sp, [3 dc in next ch-1 sp, ch 1] 9 times, join in top of beg ch 3.
**Rnd 3:** Sl st in each of next 2 dc and in next ch-1 sp; [ch 4, tr in same sp, dc in next ch-1 sp, *ch 6, sl st in 6th ch from hook for picot, sl st in last dc made,* tr in next ch-1 sp, ch 4, sl st in same sp] 5 times. Fasten off.

## *Star #12* ►

Approximately 2¼″ diameter

### *Materials*
DMC Cebelia #20, 8 yds.
Size 10 steel crochet hook.

Ch 9; join with sl st in first ch to form ring.
**Rnd 1:** Ch 2; work 19 hdc in ring, join in top of beg ch 2.
**Rnd 2:** [Ch 10, sc in next sc] 19 times; ch 4, dtr in base of beg ch 10—20 lps.
**Rnd 3:** Ch 3, tr around dtr just made, *ch 3, sl st in 3rd ch from hook for picot,* tr around same dtr, ch 3, sl st in same sp, sl st in next lp; *ch 3, tr in same lp, work picot, tr in lp, ch 3, sl st in same lp, sl st in next lp. Rep from * 18 times, ending last rep with sl st in base of beg ch 3. Fasten off.

## ◄ *Star #13*

Approximately 3½″ diameter

### *Materials*
DMC Cebelia #10, 11 yds.
Size 7 steel crochet hook.

Ch 12; join with sl st in first ch to form ring.
**Rnd 1:** Ch 3, work 29 dc in ring; join in top of beg ch 3.
**Rnd 2:** Ch 5 (counts as dtr), dtr in next dc, ch 4, [dtr in each of next 2 dc, ch 4] 14 times; join in top of beg ch 5.
**Rnd 3:** Sc in sp before next dtr, †*[ch 9, sl st in 9th ch from hook for large picot] 5 times, sl st in first picot made, sc in same sp as last sc, [4 sc in next ch-4 sp] 3 times,* sc bet next 2 dtr. Rep from † 3 times, rep bet *s, sl st in first sc of rnd. Fasten off.

### ◄ Star #14

Approximately 1¾″ diameter

**Materials**
DMC Cebelia #20, 3½ yds.
Size 10 steel crochet hook.

Ch 7; join with sl st in first ch to form ring.
**Rnd 1:** *Sc in ring, ch 7, sc in ring, ch 12; rep from * 4 times, join in first sc.
**Rnd 2:** Sl st to top of next ch-7 lp, *sc in top of ch-7 lp, *ch 3, sl st in 3rd ch from hook for small picot*, sc in same lp, work 2 small picots, sc in top of next ch-12 lp, *ch 6, sl st in 6th ch from hook for large picot*, sc in same lp, work 2 small picots. Rep from * 4 times; join in first sc. Fasten off.

### Star #15 ►

Approximately 3½″ diameter

**Materials**
DMC Cebelia #10, 11½ yds.
Size 7 steel crochet hook.

Ch 30; join with sl st in first ch to form ring.
**Rnd 1:** Ch 3 (counts as dc), [2 dc in next ch, dc in next ch] 14 times, 2 dc in next ch, join in top of beg ch 3—45 dc.
**Rnd 2:** [Sc in next st, hdc in next st, dc in next st, tr in next st, 5 dtr in next st, tr in next st, dc in next st, hdc in next st, sc in next st] 5 times; join in first st.
**Rnd 3:** Sc in same sp and in each of next 4 sts, *hdc in next st, ch 2, in next st work dc, ch 2, tr, ch 2, dc and ch 2; hdc in next st, sc in each of next 10 sts. Rep from * 4 times, ending last rep with sc in each of next 5 sts, join in first st. Fasten off.

### ◄ Star #16

Approximately 2″ diameter

**Materials**
DMC pearl cotton #5, 3 yds.
Size 4 steel crochet hook.

Ch 7; join with sl st in first ch to form ring.
**Rnd 1:** Work 15 sc in ring; join in first sc.
**Rnd 2:** Sc in same sp as sl st, [sc in each of next 2 sc, *ch 5, sl st in 5th ch from hook for picot*, sc in last sc worked in, sc in next sc] 4 times, sc in next sc, work sc, picot and sc in next sc; join in first sc.
**Rnd 3:** Sc in next sc, *ch 7, work picot, ch 7, skip picot and 2 sc, sc in next sc; rep from *, ending last rep skip picot and 2 sc, sl st in first sc of rnd. Fasten off.

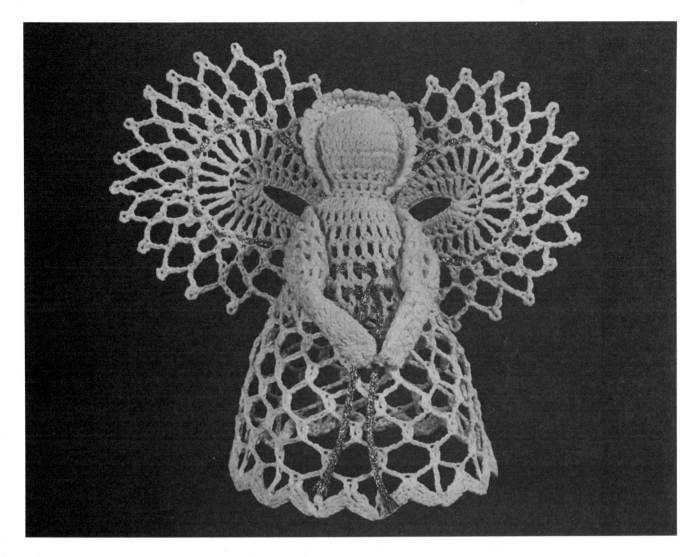

## ▲ *Angel #1*

Approximately 4″ diameter at lower edge; 6½″ high

### *Materials*
DMC #5 pearl cotton, 80 yds.
Size 4 steel crochet hook.
48″ Balger ⅛″-wide ribbon.
Small amount polyester stuffing.

### *Head and Body*
Ch 5; join with sl st in first ch to form ring.
**Rnd 1:** Work 9 sc in ring; join in first sc of rnd.
**Rnd 2:** 2 sc in same sp, 2 sc in each remaining sc around; join in first sc of rnd—18 sc.
**Rnd 3:** Ch 2 (counts as hdc); hdc in same sp, 2 hdc in next sp, hdc in next sp, [2 hdc in each of next 2 sps, hdc in next sp] 5 times, join in top of beg ch 2—30 sts.
**Rnds 4–6:** Ch 3, dc in each dc around; join in top of beg ch 3.
**Rnd 7:** Ch 3, skip next dc, [dc in next dc, skip next dc] 14 times—15 sts. Stuff head.
**Rnds 8 & 9:** Ch 2, hdc in next st and in each st around; join in top of beg ch 2.
**Halo:** Working in bars of rows, work 11 or 12 sc up head, work ch 3 over beg ring, work same number of sc down head to Rnd 9; turn. Sc in each sc, working 2 sc in ch-3 sp; turn. Sl st in first sc, sc in each sc to last sc, sl st in last sc; turn. Sl st in first sc, [sc in next sc, *ch 3, sl st in first ch for picot*] across, sl st in last sc. Sl st to last st of Rnd 9.
**Rnd 10:** Continuing around Rnd 9, ch 3, dc in same sp, 2 dc in each of next 14 sc, join in top of beg ch 3—30 sts.
**Rnd 11:** Ch 3, dc in each dc; join in top of beg ch 3.

**Rnd 12:** Ch 4 (counts as dc and ch 1), [dc in next dc, ch 1] 29 times; join in 3rd ch of beg ch 4.
**Rnd 13:** Ch 4, skip next ch-1 sp, [dc in next dc, ch 1, skip next ch-1 sp] 29 times; join in 3rd ch of beg ch 4.
**Rnds 14 & 15:** Ch 5 (counts as dc and ch 2), skip next ch-sp, [dc in next dc, ch 2, skip next ch-sp] 29 times; join in 3rd ch of beg ch 5.
**Rnd 16:** Ch 4 (counts as hdc and ch 2), skip next ch-2 sp, [hdc in next dc, ch 2, skip next ch-2 sp] 29 times; join in 2nd ch of beg ch 4.
**Rnd 17:** Sc in same sp, ch 2, *ch 5, sl st in 5th ch from hook for large picot*, ch 2, skip next ch-2 sp, hdc and ch-2 sp, [sc in next hdc, ch 2, work large picot, ch 2, skip next ch-2 sp, hdc and ch-2 sp] 14 times; join in first sc.
**Rnds 18–22:** Sl st to top of first large picot, sc in same sp, [ch 3, work large picot, ch 3, sc in next large picot] 15 times, ending last rep with sl st in first sc of rnd.
**Rnd 23:** Ch 4, tr in next picot, ch 4, sl st in same sp, [ch 4, tr in same sp, tr in sc over large picot of Rnd 21, tr in next picot, ch 4, sl st in same sp] 14 times, ch 4, tr in same sp, join in top of beg ch 4.
**Rnd 24:** [Ch 5, skip next tr and ch-4 sp, sl st in next sl st, ch 5, skip next ch-4 sp and tr, sl st in next tr] 15 times, ending last rep with sl st in joining of previous rnd. Fasten off.

### *Wings* (make 2)
Ch 20; join with sl st in first ch to form ring.
**Rnd 1:** Working in each ch, sc in same sp and in each of next 2 chs, hdc in 3 chs, dc in 3, 3 tr in each of next 2 chs, dc in 3 chs, hdc in 3, sc in 3; join in first sc.
**Rnd 2:** Sc in same sp, ch 1, [sc in next st, ch 1] twice, [hdc in

29

next st, ch 1] 3 times, [dc in next st, ch 1] 3 times, [tr, ch 1, tr, ch 1 all in next st] 6 times, [dc in next st, ch 1] 3 times, [hdc in next st, ch 1] 3 times, [sc in next st, ch 1] twice, sc in last sc, sl st in first sc.

**Rnd 3:** Sc in same sp, sc in ch-1 sp, *[ch 1, *ch 3, sl st in first ch for small picot*, ch 1, skip next sc, ch-1 sp and sc, sc in next ch-1 sp] 4 times*, [ch 1, work small picot, ch 1, sc in ch 1] 12 times, rep bet *s, sc in sc, join in first sc.

**Rnd 4:** Sc in same sp and in next sc, [ch 3, sc in next picot] twice, [ch 3, work small picot, ch 3, sc in small picot] 17 times, ch 3, sc in next small picot, ch 3, sc in each of 2 sc, join in first sc.

**Rnd 5:** Sc in same sp and in next sc, [2 sc in ch-3 sp, sc in next sc] twice, ch 3, sc in next picot, [ch 3, *ch 5, sl st in 5th ch from hook for large picot*, ch 3, sc in next small picot] 16 times, ch 3, sc in next sc, [2 sc in next ch-3 sp, sc in next sc] twice, sc in next sc, join in first sc. Fasten off.

*Arms* (make 2)
Starting at shoulder, ch 7; join with sl st in first ch to form ring.
**Rnd 1:** Ch 1, 10 sc in ring; join.
**Rnd 2:** Ch 3 (counts as hdc and ch 1), [hdc in next st, ch 1] 9 times, join in 2nd ch of ch 3.
**Rnds 3–7:** Ch 5 (counts as dc and ch 2), [skip next ch-sp, dc in next hdc, ch 2] 9 times, skip next ch-sp, join in 3rd ch of ch 5.
**Rnd 8:** Working in back lps only, sc in each dc; join—10 sc.
**Rnd 9:** Ch 3, sc in 9 sc, join in top of beg ch 3.
**Rnds 10–12:** Ch 3, dc in each dc, join in top of beg ch 3.
**Rnd 13:** Ch 3, [yo, draw up a lp in next st, yo and draw through 2 lps] 3 times, yo and draw through all lps on hook for decrease; rep decrease twice, join in top of beg ch 3. Fasten off.

Cut ribbon into one 24″ length and two 12″ lengths. Thread a short length of ribbon through Rnd 3 of each wing; tie bow at bottom. Thread remaining ribbon through Rnds 15 and 16 of body; tie in front. Sew arms to Rnds 12–13 of body, toward back; tack hands together. Sew wings to back of angel on Rnds 12, 13 and 14. Tack top picots together to join and shape wings.

## ▲ *Angel #2*

Approximately 2¾″ diameter at lower edge, 5″ high

### *Materials*
DMC Cebelia #20, 92 yds.
Size 10 steel crochet hook.
Balger ⅛″-wide ribbon—1 yd. each two different colors.
Small amount polyester stuffing.

### *Head and Body*
Starting at top of head, ch 6; join with with sl st in first ch to form ring.
**Rnd 1:** Ch 2, work 11 hdc in ring, join in top of beg ch 2.
**Rnd 2:** Ch 2, hdc in same sp, 2 hdc in each remaining hdc—24 hdc.
**Rnd 3:** Working in front lps of sts, sc in same sp, [*ch 4, sl st in first ch for picot*, sc in each of next 2 hdc] 11 times, work picot, sc in last hdc, join in first sc.
**Rnd 4:** Sl st to back lp of first st of Rnd 2; ch 2, working in back lps, hdc in each remaining hdc around; join in top of beg ch 2.
**Rnds 5–9:** Working in both lps of sts, ch 2, hdc in each hdc around; join in top of beg ch 2—24 hdc.
**Rnd 10:** [Sc in each of next 2 hdc, skip next hdc] 8 times; join in first sc—16 sc. Stuff head.
**Rnds 11 & 12:** Sc in each sc around; join in first sc.
**Rnd 13:** Ch 4 (counts as dc and ch 1), [dc in next sc, ch 1] 15 times; join in 3rd ch of beg ch 4.
**Rnds 14 & 15:** Ch 5 (counts as dc and ch 2), [dc in next dc, ch 2] 15 times; join in 3rd ch of beg ch 4.
**Rnd 16:** Ch 3 (counts as dc), dc in same sp, ch 2, dc in next dc, ch 2, [2 dc in next dc, ch 2, dc in next dc, ch 2] 7 times, join in top of beg ch 3.
**Rnd 17:** Sl st in sp before next dc, ch 3, dc in same sp, ch 2, skip ch-2 sp, 2 dc in next dc, ch 2, [skip ch-2 sp, 2 dc *bet* next 2 dc, ch 2, skip ch-2 sp, 2 dc in next dc, ch 2] 7 times; join in top of beg ch 3.
**Rnds 18–21:** Sl st in sp before next dc, ch 3, dc in same sp, ch 3,

skip ch-2 sp, [2 dc bet next 2 dc, ch 2, skip ch-2 sp] 15 times; join in top of beg ch 3.

**Rnd 22:** Sl st in sp before next dc, ch 6 (counts as dc and ch 3), skip ch-2 sp, [dc bet next 2 dc, ch 3, skip ch-2 sp] 15 times, join in 3rd ch of beg ch 6.

**Rnds 23–28:** Ch 7 (counts as dc and ch 4), [dc in next dc, ch 4] 15 times; join in 3rd ch of beg ch 7.

**Rnd 29:** Ch 6 (counts as dc and ch 3), [dc in same sp, ch 3] twice, *in next dc, work [dc, ch 3] 3 times; rep from * around, join in 3rd ch of beg ch 3.

**Rnd 30:** Sl st to center of first ch-3 sp, sc in same sp, ch 3, *sc in next ch-3 sp, ch 3; rep from * around; join in 3rd ch of beg ch 3. Fasten off.

### Flowers (make 6)
Ch 5; join with sl st in first ch to form ring.

**Rnd 1:** Ch 1, 6 hdc in ring; join in first hdc.

**Rnd 2:** Working in front lps only, work sc, dc and sc in each hdc around; join in first sc.

**Rnd 3:** Working in back lps of Rnd 1 sts, work sl st, ch 3, 2 dc, ch 3 and sl st in each st around. Fasten off, leaving several inches of thread. Tie flowers evenly spaced around skirt, just above ruffle.

### Wings (make 2)
Ch 15.

**Rnd 1:** Sc in 2nd ch from hook, *hdc in 2 chs, dc in 2 chs, tr in 4 chs, dc in 2 chs, hdc in 2 chs*, 3 sc in last ch. Continuing around opposite side of ch, rep bet *s, 2 sc in same sp as first sc of rnd; join in first sc.

**Rnd 2:** Ch 4 (counts as dc and ch 1), work dc and ch 1 in each st around; join in 3rd of beg ch 4.

**Rnds 3 & 4:** Ch 5 (counts as dc and ch 2), work dc and ch 2 in each dc around; join in 3rd ch of beg ch 5.

**Rnd 5:** [Sc in next dc, sc in next ch-2 sp, work picot, sc in sc just made] 30 times; join in first sc. Fasten off.

### Arms (make 2)
Starting at shoulder, ch 6; join with sl st in first ch to form ring.

**Rnd 1:** Ch 4, work 11 tr in ring; join in top of beg ch 4.

**Rnds 2–5:** Ch 4, tr in each tr around; join in top of beg ch 4.

**Rnd 6:** Working in front lps only, ch 5 (counts as tr and ch 1), tr in same sp, ch 1, [work tr, ch 1, tr and ch 1 in next tr] 11 times; join in 4th ch of beg ch 5.

**Rnd 7:** Sl st down ch 3 to back lp of first st of Rnd 5, ch 2; working in back lps, hdc in each hdc around; join in top of beg ch 2.

**Rnd 8:** Ch 2, hdc in each of next 2 hdc, skip next hdc, [hdc in each of next 3 hdc, skip next hdc] twice; join in top of beg ch 2—9 hdc.

**Rnds 9 & 10:** Ch 2, hdc in each hdc around; join in top of beg ch 2.

**Rnd 11:** [Sc in next hdc, skip next hdc] 4 times, sc in last hdc; join in first sc. Fasten off, leaving about 4″. Sew opening closed.

Cut each ribbon into three 12″-strands. Thread a strand through Rnd 3 of each wing; thread a different color strand through Rnd 4. Tie all ends in a bow at bottom. Sew arms to sides of body on Rnds 14–15; tack hands together. Sew wings to back at Rnds 13–16. Tie remaining ribbon around neck.

---

# Angel #3

Approximately 3¼″ diameter at lower edge, 6½″ high

### Materials
DMC Cebelia #10, 110 yds.
Size 7 steel crochet hook.
60″ Balger ⅛″-wide ribbon.
Small amount polyester stuffing.

### Head and Body
Starting at the top of the head, ch 5; join with sl st in first ch to form ring.

**Rnd 1:** 10 sc in ring; join in first sc.

**Rnd 2:** Ch 3 (counts as dc), dc in same sc, 2 dc in each sc around; join in top of beg ch 3—20 dc.

**Rnd 3:** Ch 2, hdc in each dc around; join in top of beg ch 2.

**Rnd 4—Halo:** Working in front lps only of Rnd 3 sts, sc in same st, 2 sc in next sc, [sc in next sc, 2 sc in next sc] 9 times; join in first sc—30 sc.

**Rnd 5:** Working in both lps of sts, sc in same st, sc in next st, *ch 3, sl st in 3rd ch from hook for small picot*, [sc in each of next 2 sts, work small picot] 14 times; join in first sc.

**Rnd 6:** Sl st to back lp of first st of Rnd 3. Working in back lps, ch 2, hdc in each of next 2 sts, 2 hdc in next st, [hdc in each of next 3 sts, 2 hdc in next st] 4 times; join in top of beg ch 2—25 hdc.

**Rnds 7–10:** Working in both lps of sts, ch 2, hdc in each st around; join in top of beg ch 2. Stuff head at end of Rnd 10.

**Rnd 11:** Sc in same sp as joining; [sc in next st, skip next st] 12 times; join in first sc—13 sc.

**Rnds 12 & 13:** Sc in each sc; join in first sc.

**Rnd 14:** Ch 3, dc in same sp, 2 dc in each dc around; join in top of beg ch 3—26 dc.

**Rnd 15:** *Ch 2, [ch 4, sl st in 4th ch from hook for large picot] 3

times, sl st in base of first large picot—picot group made, ch 3, skip next dc, sl st in next dc. Rep from * 12 times—13 picot groups.

**Rnds 16 & 17:** Sl st to center back of next picot group; [ch 3, work picot group as before, ch 3, sl st in center back of next picot group] 13 times.

**Rnd 18:** Sl st to center back of next picot group, [ch 4, work picot group, ch 4, sl st in center back of next picot group] 13 times.

**Rnd 19:** Sl st to center back of next picot group, [ch 5, work picot group, ch 5, sl st in center back of next picot group] 13 times.

**Rnd 20:** Sl st to center back of next picot group, [ch 6, work picot group, ch 6, sl st in center back of next picot group] 13 times.

**Rnd 21:** Sl st to center back of next picot group, [ch 5, sl st in center back of next picot group] 13 times.

**Rnd 22:** In each ch-5 loop, work sc, hdc, dc, tr, dc, hdc and sc; join in first sc.

**Rnd 23:** Ch 4 (counts as dc and ch 1); drawing all sts up to same level so rnd is even across top, *skip next st, dc in next st, ch 1; rep from * around, ending last rep with ch 1, join in 3rd ch of beg ch 4.

**Rnd 24:** Ch 5 (counts as dc and ch 2), work dc and ch 2 in each dc around; join in 3rd ch of beg ch 5.

**Rnd 25:** Work sc and ch 1 in each dc around; join in first sc. Fasten off.

### Wings (make 2)
Ch 11.

**Row 1:** Dc in 4th ch from hook and in each remaining ch—9 dc, counting beg ch 3.

**Row 2:** Ch 3, turn, dc in each dc across.

**Row 3:** Ch 3, turn, dc in same sp, [ch 1, skip next dc, dc in next dc] 3 times, ch 1, 2 dc in top of beg ch 3.

**Row 4:** Ch 3, turn, dc in same sp, dc in next dc, [ch 1, skip next

dc, tr in next dc] 3 times, ch 1, dc in next dc, 2 dc in top of beg ch 3.

**Row 5:** Ch 3, turn, dc in same sp, dc in each of next 2 dc, [dc in ch-1 sp, dc in next tr] 3 times, dc in next ch-1 sp, dc in each of next 2 dc, 2 dc in top of beg ch 3—15 sts.

**Row 6:** *Ch 1,* turn, 2 sc in first st, sc in next st, hdc in each of next 2 sts, dc in each of next 2 sts, tr in each of next 3 sts, dc in each of next 2 sts, hdc in each of next 2 sts, sc in next st, 2 sc in top of beg ch 3—17 sts.

**Row 7:** Ch 1, turn, [ch 3, skip next st, sc in next st] 8 times.

**Row 8:** Ch 4, turn, [sc in next ch-3 sp, ch 3] 8 times, sc in last sc.

**Row 9:** Turn, sl st to center of next ch-3 sp, sc in same sp, [ch 4, sc in next ch-3 sp] 8 times.

**Row 10:** Ch 3, turn, dc in same sc, [3 dc in next ch-3 sp, dc in next dc] 8 times—34 dc.

**Row 11:** Ch 1, turn, sc in first dc, [ch 4, skip next 2 dc, sc in next dc] 10 times, ch 4, skip next 2 sc, sc in top of beg ch 3.

**Row 12:** Ch 4, turn, [sc in next ch-4 sp, ch 4] 10 times, sc in next ch-4 sp, ch 3, sc in last sc.

**Row 13:** Turn, sl st to center of next ch-sp, sc in same sp, [ch 4, sc in next ch-4 sp] 10 times, ch 4, sc in last sc.

**Row 14:** Rep Row 12.

**Row 15:** Turn, sl st to center of ch-3 sp, sc in same sp, [ch 5, sc in next ch-sp] 11 times.

**Row 16:** Ch 1, turn, [2 sc in first ch-sp, work large picot, 2 sc in same ch-sp, sc in next sc] 11 times. Continuing around wing, sc along side edge, work 2 sc in each mesh and dc row, 1 sc in each sc row and 1 sc between rows; 3 sc in bottom corner of Row 1, continue around to beg of Row 16; join in first sc of row. Fasten off.

**Arms** (make 2)

Starting at shoulder, ch 5; join with sl st in first ch to form ring.

**Rnd 1:** Ch 3, 11 dc in ring; join in top of beg ch 3.

**Rnds 2–8:** Ch 3, dc in each dc; join in top of beg ch 3.

**Rnd 9:** Ch 3, dc in each of next 2 dc, skip next dc, [dc in each of next 3 dc, skip next dc] twice, join in top of beg ch 3—9 dc.

**Rnds 10 & 11:** Ch 3, dc in each dc.

**Rnd 12:** Ch 2, hdc in next dc, skip next dc, [hdc in each of next 2 dc, skip next dc] twice, join in top of beg ch 2. Fasten off.

Beginning at front, thread a 24″ length of ribbon through 2 bottom rnds of body, tie ends in bow. Cut remaining ribbon into three 12″ lengths. Tie one strand around neck; make bow. Make bow in center of last row of each wing. Sew arms to sides of body on Rnds 15–16. Sew wings to center back on Rnds 15–17.